— A MEMOIR —

SEVEN YEARS
TO SYMONE

Finding Faith to
Overcome Infertility and
Have a Baby After 40

KIMBERLY V. GARNER

Copyright © 2020 Kimberly V. Garner
Cover Design: Steven Garner
Published by Nexcue
ISBN: 978-1-7347385-0-6

7yearstosymone.com

Dedication

To my husband, Steve.

Your love, encouragement, positivity, and consistency are everything to me. Thank you for your prayers and unwillingness to give up on our journey to become parents. You are an amazing dad and a wonderful husband. I love you honey.

To my daughter, Symone.

May you always know the power of prayer and how very special you are. Forever mommy's shugga wugga. I love you.

To my dad and stepmom, Leroy and Hannah.

Thank you for your love and support and for being the best grandparents ever. Symone is extremely blessed to have a grandmother and granddad that are very present in her life. I do not take that for granted. I love you both.

In memory of my mom, Charolette.

I am so deeply grateful for my mom's love and the beautiful relationship we shared. To be her daughter (and my dad's) is one my greatest blessings. She would have adored her granddaughter.

Acknowledgments

I believe in the power of prayer and thank God for blessing me with Symone.

I am thankful for my siblings and their spouses: Lewis and Dominque, Brandon, Craig and Pam, and Monica and Lawrence. Thank you for your love and support on our journey. My heart is full every time we are together and I see Symone having an awesome time with her uncles and aunts.

To my nephews Julian, Lucas, and Trevor....you all know how much your little cousin absolutely adores you three, her sweet baboos! Thank you for the time you all spend with her. It makes me happy to know that she has excellent role models to emulate.

And finally, I must express my gratitude to friends Karen and Kenny, Kesha and Eric, Candace and Rodney, Sonya and Michael, Nishina and Keith, Regina, Leroy, Joan, Kawanna, Anastasia and Albert, Camille and Owen, Racquel and Leslie, and to our Shiloh church family. I am forever grateful for your prayers and unwavering support while on our seven-year journey to Symone.

Contents

Introduction

I guess you can say I am a late bloomer in some areas of my life. I started school "late" because I have an October birthday. And I was older than most of my friends when I said, "I do!" Yet I never expected that becoming a mother would take the course it did. Month after month, year after year, I yearned for a baby. At times, I was mad and shed countless tears because I could not understand why my body would not cooperate, why it was not doing what it was created to do. I was so desperate to become a mommy.

My seven-year journey to motherhood was punctuated by heartache and emotional fatigue. But in all of my disappointment, I refused to accept that I could not have a child. I would not allow the emotional toll, the losses, and my proverbial maternal clock, nearing its last tick, extinguish the desire in my heart. I was meant to be a mother. Period.

Whether you are a few months into your journey or a few years, facing infertility can be a gut-wrenching and lonely feeling. I understand. You are not alone. I know the deep sense of desperation that consumes you because you feel like you're running out of time, time based on either the timetable you created for your life or your stubborn biological clock—I entered my forties still longing to have a baby. I know the fear that grips you at the thought of having yet another miscarriage or stillbirth. I am all too familiar with the feelings of guilt and responsibility that subtly creep in when thinking about your husband's dream of fatherhood. I understand the internal struggle between your mind telling you it simply is not going to happen and your heart unwilling to let go of the possibility that it could— even in those moments when the emptiness of your womb is almost unbearable. But I also know, without a doubt, that I would not have Symone if I had given up!

After meeting women on this journey and friends asking me to encourage their friends struggling with infertility, not only did I want to write my story to inspire future moms-to-be, I had to write it. As challenging as it was, my experience is a testament to the unspeakable joy that can result from finding faith to not give up regardless of your circumstances or how you feel. Symone is a gift! And in my gratitude and thankfulness, I am passionate about inspiring women who feel like I once felt to fight for their fertility, in faith.

I do not know where you are on your journey. If you are weary, if you are feeling helpless or hopeless, let my story encourage you. God can do anything!

CHAPTER ONE

Mr. Right

I must say, I thoroughly enjoyed my childhood. I am the only girl in my immediate family. While I was not afraid to get dirty, and wrestling with my dad was practically a nightly ritual, I was undeniably a girly girl. I took baton lessons and modeled for a department store. I took dance classes for years, so leotards, ballet shoes, and tutus were wardrobe staples. I even went to charm school at a store in our local shopping mall. Yes, I said charm school. My parents hoped the classes would boost my self-confidence given my shy tendencies when meeting people. I learned about proper etiquette, everything from how to introduce myself and speak in front of others to how to set the table.

Growing up, I knew I was special to my parents. They hugged and kissed me every day and were intentional about telling me they loved me. I dreamt that I would get married one day and have kids who I would love and pour into like my parents did. Although I had boyfriends in high school, I certainly never thought about marrying any of them. I was idealistic and assumed I would meet my husband when I went to college. He would be intelligent and articulate, like my dad, and definitely a cutie. But that did not happen. A year after I graduated from college, I went to law school and anticipated meeting him there. Instead, I met a guy in medical school who I dated exclusively for several years after I finished law school. I was certain that he was "Mr. Right." He was a Christian, he was smart, and we had fun hanging out together and with our crew of friends. But we eventually broke up. *Now what?* I thought. By this time, I was twenty-nine and beginning to get a bit anxious. I was ready to meet my husband, and there were no prospects . . . or so I thought.

While dating said medical student, I began attending church regularly with him. He lived in another city about ninety miles from me. After we stopped dating, I started visiting a church closer to home. I knew one person there and sat with her each week. It is at this church where I met him, my future husband.

God answered my prayers. I had earnestly prayed for a

God-fearing, intelligent, attractive, loving, fun, and outgoing husband. I even prayed that he would not already be a dad because I wanted us to share that experience together. I wanted my first baby to be his first baby. As I said, God answered my prayers. We dated for nearly three years before I said, "I do!" to my wonderful husband, Steve. Despite being in my early thirties when we wed, I was in no rush to start a family. I figured I had time. Besides, I wanted to enjoy my new role as Mrs. Garner.

Trust in the LORD with all your heart and lean not on your own understanding; in all your ways submit to him, and he will make your paths straight.

— PROVERBS 3:5-6

CHAPTER TWO

Shattered

I remember it was a Thursday morning. I was glued to my computer screen, reviewing something, like always, and noticed some movement in my peripheral vision. My manager paused at the entrance of my cubicle and just stood there, without saying a word at first. That was unusual because he is normally chatty and quite comical. He hesitantly broke his brief silence and whispered, "Your husband is downstairs." I knew why he was there.

Immediately, I became nauseated and labored to breathe as I logged off my computer and gathered my things. My manager asked if I needed any help and offered to accompany me to the lobby. In a crackling voice, I declined the invitation. Soon, my vision blurred from the tears that began to well up in my eyes. I could not believe that the woman I had known my entire life, the woman who gave me life and who I could not imagine living without, had died. My beautiful mom had been diagnosed with cancer fifteen years earlier. At that time, she had a lumpectomy and underwent radiation treatment which put her in remission for years. But the cancer returned that summer and quickly spread throughout her body, including to her brain. It had taken her life. I was stunned.

My mom was my everything. She was my favorite playmate as a little girl. And as I got older, she became my best friend; my one true confidante; my shopping partner; my cheerleader. People used to say we sounded alike. As I have grown older, I can hear her voice in mine. Many often remarked that I looked just like my mom, with the exception of her fair complexion. In fact, when I was younger, she would bring me to work with her in the summers because she was the executive director of a community center for youth, and her co-workers would call me little Charolette. But her nickname for me was shugga wugga, something she called me well beyond my childhood. Our bond was incredibly special and irreplaceable.

My mom died one month and two days before my thirty-fourth birthday. While I was quickly approaching what the medical profession calls advance maternal age (i.e., thirty-five and older) there was no way I could even think about having a baby at that time. My life had been forever changed, and now I was forced to figure out how to navigate the rest of it without Charolette Uvon Miller—my beautiful mom.

Children are a heritage from the LORD, offspring a reward from him.

— PSALM 127:3

CHAPTER THREE

Getting Pregnant is Supposed to be Easy, Right?!

YEAR ONE

S lowly, a year and a half passed after losing my mom, and I do not know how I survived. Well, I take that back. I know God carried me, friends prayed for me, and my husband, a bonafide man of God, comforted me and covered me in prayer. Even with all of this support, the pain of my loss was still very acute.

By this time I was almost thirty-six, and we had spent the last few months trying to get pregnant. I was consistently tracking my menstrual cycle. I measured and charted my body basal temperature to know when I was ovulating, making sure we were intimate at the optimal time. Sometimes I would even lie on the bed with my legs in the air after being intimate, hoping a sperm would collide into one of my eggs. I was on a mission to become a mom and did not care how I looked in the process.

We continued trying to conceive for more than half a year. At three months shy of my thirty-seventh birthday, my proverbial maternal clock no longer sounded like an unalarming tick. It suddenly became like a loud Bong, reminding me that time was of the essence if I was going to bear a child, and I was in full anxious mode! So in late summer, I had my first prenatal visit with a new OB-GYN. I was so blessed to meet her. She was and still is an awesome doctor. Her bedside manners are par excellence. She recommended we try a few rounds of clomiphene citrate, an oral medication used to treat certain types of female infertility. This was the "easiest" and most cost-efficient infertility treatment option so we proceeded without hesitation. I was on clomiphene citrate for three months with no success. In the meantime, my OB was enjoying her second pregnancy and her baby bump grew a little more each time I saw her.

Considering my age, she urged us to seriously think about seeing a fertility specialist. Steve and I agreed that would be our next step and scheduled an appointment with one that following February. We discussed all the options and attendant costs—our insurance did not cover fertility treatments—

and decided to start with intrauterine insemination (IUI) treatments. I thought, *The doc is shooting my husband's sperm directly into my uterus. Surely, this has to work! A woman's egg unites with a man's sperm everyday all over the world. So why wouldn't my husband's freshly scrubbed sperm not collide into at least one of my eggs?*

Nothing happened.

He gives strength to the weary and increases the power of the weak.

— ISAIAH 40:29

CHAPTER FOUR

From Love to Loss

YEAR TWO – YEAR THREE

I n October of that same year, we bit the financial and emotional bullet and entered the world of in vitro fertilization (IVF). This pricey world of doctors and self-administered shots, lots of appointments, checks, ultrasounds, physical discomfort, and worrying—all occurring for months during a single IVF cycle—is not for the faint of heart. The most daunting part of this process was probably giving myself shots and the emotional holding pattern I found myself in while waiting for results. But the cost of the procedure was a close second since our insurance did not cover fertility treatments. Did I mention IVF treatments are expensive?! Administering the shots was inconvenient sometimes. There were afternoons we would be at our friends' home, a couple who knew we were having treatments, when I had to inject the infertility medicine. I kept the needle in my purse and refrigerated the medicine while there. When it was time, regardless of what I was doing at that moment, I would cease my present activity to give myself that shot. For my squeamish self, poking below my belly button required me to overcome a major mental hurdle . . . I hated it! And, before beginning IVF treatments, Steve and I had to attend genetic counseling where the counselor shared ALL the negative statistics about older women having healthy babies. The counseling was depressing and terrifying. But I knew God had given me the desire to be a mother, and the loss of my mom only intensified my yearning. I was meant to be a mother.

After the nearly three-month period of one IVF cycle, Bingo, we were preggo! We could not believe it. My mind raced into overdrive: *Please God, bless me with a healthy daughter! I want to have the type of relationship with her that I had with my mom. Who will she look like? Time to start shopping, thinking about the registry . . .*

Because I was nervous after hearing the bleak picture painted by the genetic counselor, I began meditating on God's promises and answered prayers for children. I inundated my heart and mind with His Word to strengthen my belief that

He really can do anything, including allowing me to give birth.

Again, because of my age—thirty-eight by this time—we followed the recommendation to have an amniocentesis procedure. This procedure is used in prenatal diagnoses of chromosomal abnormalities and fetal infections and can reveal the baby's gender. I didn't know anyone who had this procedure and hadn't acquainted myself with what was involved. In other words, I wasn't prepared physically or mentally for the pain! The doctor slowly inserted a long, thin needle through my abdomen and uterus to remove a small amount of amniotic fluid. I cannot put into words how painful the procedure was. I held my breath and gripped the exam table like my life depended on it, almost falling off of it during the procedure. The doctor secured the sample and removed the needle and asked how I was feeling. "Okay," I mumbled. But I was not okay; I was in pain and trying to detach myself from that awful experience. I was in no mood to chat.

We had to wait weeks for the test results. And for some reason, our results were delayed several days beyond when we were told we would receive them. Then on Valentine's Day, I received the call . . . we were having a girl! I was absolutely elated. I was going to have a daughter, and I would be able to have that mommy-daughter relationship with her that I had with my mom. I was twelve weeks pregnant and could not wait to meet her.

However, on the heels of my joy came not-so-good news. The results of the amniocentesis revealed that there was some thickness around my daughter's neck, which was an indication of heart problems. In addition, one of the ultrasounds showed a few of her digits had not developed. My stomach sank. This was not what I expected. I tried to continue to stand on God's promises and claim victory over my pregnancy in the name of Jesus! I was scared but fighting my fear with God's Word.

Several weeks later on March ninth, I was at my twenty-week prenatal appointment, lying on the exam table. My doctor listened for a heartbeat, but could not find it. She remained calm because she had to "search" for my daughter's heartbeat at my last appointment. After several more minutes of gliding the transducer across my uterus, we took a quick stroll down the hall to another room to have her sonogram technician perform a sonogram. My heart was racing. After I got on the exam table, I was nervously asking the technician if everything was okay. Silence.

Seconds later, I vividly remember slowly turning my head to

the right to peer at the monitor. I was stunned. My daughter was not moving, she was completely still, appearing to be suspended in mid- air. As I turned my head back around, my doctor exclaimed, "I am so sorry Kim!" I cried out, "No, no . . . I can't believe it! I can't believe it!" My doctor embraced me in her arms as I began to sob uncontrollably. By this date, I was already in love with my daughter. I had started registering for my baby shower because I was so excited to prepare for and meet her. My co-workers knew I was pregnant. I had already taken so many baby bump pictures, and I was wearing maternity clothes at that appointment. Just two days earlier, my husband had left his former employer to accept a position at his current job. His former co-workers gave him a goodbye gift—the baby swing from our baby registry!

After thirty minutes or so, I was able to halfway pull myself together. While still weeping and sniffling, I called Steve with the devastating news, "I am at my doctor's appointment . . . they did an ultrasound and the baby wasn't moving . . . she's not alive." I distinctly remember not being able to utter the words "died" or "dead." I think I couldn't handle the finality of what was happening in that moment. At first, he didn't understand me, and he sounded confused by what I had just described.

I continued to fumble through my words, trying to tell him what happened. I don't recall what I said before we hung up.

Next, I called my dad. He did not answer, so I called my stepmom. My doctor was still holding me as I explained to my stepmom what happened. She asked where my doctor was located and said she was on her way. I then called several of my girlfriends, fumbling over my words as I was trying to explain what happened. They seemed to be in as much disbelief as me and three of them said they would meet me at our house. My stepmom finally arrived. I could hear the nurse outside the exam room telling her where we were. She peeked into the room to make sure she was in the right place. As soon as our eyes locked, she ran to me, and I shifted from my doctor's arms to her arms. I cried a bit longer and then she said she would drive me home. The ride home was a blur, except I remember feeling sick. Throughout my pregnancy, I had terrible morning sickness. In fact, I had lost ten pounds because I simply could not eat. The sick feeling on the ride home was emotional and physical; I was in complete shock and disbelief. After all we had been through to get pregnant, I could not belief this was happening.

Shortly after we got to my house, Karen, Regina, and Racquel came, as promised, and immediately started preparing food. My dad, grandmother, and younger brother soon arrived. I do not remember when Steve got home or what we said to each other. But by the time he arrived, our home was filled with supportive friends and family trying to help us grapple with the devastating loss. Later, in the midst of tears and hugs, I realized my husband was not downstairs with everyone, but upstairs alone. I was concerned and asked Regina to check on him. She was upstairs awhile. When she came back down, she said he was okay, that he had been praying and meditating and just trying to cope. The care and love of our friends that day and the days that followed was simply amazing. My dear friend Camille even flew in town the day after our loss to be with us.

Hours after being home, I received a call. I had forgotten that one of my friends was scheduled for a sonogram that day to find out what she was having. She, another friend, and I had all been pregnant at the same time. The three of us had even taken a picture together, happily assuming that ubiquitous pregnancy pose where one hand rests on the top of your baby bump and the other cradles the bottom of it. With all the commotion of that day, I had not talked to her, so she called not knowing about our loss. I answered, sniffling and weeping a little. My friend asked what was wrong, and I told her. She was at a loss for words, surprised by what happened. I told her that I just remembered her sonogram that day and asked what she was having. "A girl," she said faintly. I congratulated her. I felt her sympathy, it was all in her voice as she told me how sorry she was for us.

Based on how far along I was in my pregnancy, my OB told me I would have to go to the hospital to "deliver" the baby. The delivery was scheduled for Monday, three days after learning our daughter had died in utero. We had to be at the hospital around 1:00 a.m.

The delivery was emotionally and physically agonizing. I had to be induced and was in labor for over twelve hours. I was given two epidurals because I could not tolerate the pain, and I had to be assisted to the bathroom multiple times, too numb and weak to walk on my own. As if the situation was not awful enough, at one point during labor, my doctor leaned over and, in a soft voice, whispered that I needed to have a blood transfusion because I had lost a lot of blood. I looked her directly in her eyes and asked, in all seriousness, if I was going to die. She insisted that I would be okay, that the blood had been screened and was safe for transfusion. This experience was totally unfathomable!

Not only was I in the hospital preparing to deliver my daughter who had died in my womb, now I needed to have a blood transfusion. The timing of the blood transfusion is hazy. I'm not sure when it occurred but recall wanting the entire ordeal to be over—the labor, the transfusion, the delivery, the emotional pain, all of it. Following the transfusion, I was in labor for a few more hours. At one point, I thought, *If my OB comes back in my room and tells me I must have a C-section, I will need to be checked into the psychiatry wing.* Thankfully, I did not have to endure that trauma. Eventually, I started to feel some pressure in my pelvic area. Exhausted and weak, I told her I felt like I needed to push. She took a look at me and told me to start pushing. Seconds later, I delivered our daughter.

I had a few close friends in the hospital throughout the day. But once it was time to deliver our daughter, only my family was in my room. They were surrounding me, standing next to and at the foot of my hospital bed.

Speaking of family, my older brother and his family from Texas had been trying to plan a summer vacation a few weeks before we found out about our loss. He said nothing was working out with regard to flights, hotels, etc. And that was unusual considering my sister-in-law works for an airline and my brother travels for his job. When he got the call from our dad about our loss, he said that was the reason things were not working out . . . God knew he needed to be with us during this difficult time. I was so grateful they were there.

Steve sat by my hospital bed the entire time, caressing my hair and asking me how I was feeling. He also had been meditating and reading the Bible, seeking encouragement and a name for our daughter. After I delivered her, my OB asked if we had a name. "Yes," he said, "Asya." Pronounced AHS-YAH, it is an African name that means born at a time of grief, symbolizing the despair we felt at delivering our stillborn baby girl.

Initially, I distinctly observed the silence in my hospital room after the stillbirth. The depressed mood in my room was in stark contrast to the grunts and muffled yelling from the mom in labor in a nearby room, sounds soon replaced by the cry of her newborn baby and the celebration of those in her room witnessing the miracle of birth. The only crying in my room came from my family who was meeting and then saying goodbye to our daughter. I remember lying there, seeing my dad crying at the foot of my bed while holding his stillborn granddaughter—his first. Then I saw Steve holding her and crying while my doctor tried to console him. That was such a painful sight. It was hard to wrap my head around everything. It was as though I was watching someone else go through this horrible experience. But it was not someone else. It was me. Unlike my family, I could not hold her. I knew I could not handle remembering that feeling of cradling her tiny lifeless body in my arms, her small head resting in the bent of my arm. It was just too much. The guilt of not holding her was mitigated by the fact that her dad and grandparents held and kissed her. I recall staring at all of them with a few tears rolling down my face; I was not sobbing like I had in the doctor's office three days earlier. I quietly wept as my dream of motherhood slowly unraveled before me, watching this unimaginable scene unfold. I was having what felt like an out-of-body experience. I still couldn't believe what had happened.

The nurse took Asya in another room for a photo shoot of sorts. My doctor wanted to make sure we had pictures of her. At twenty weeks, some of her facial features had begun to form. Steve said that she looked like me. He was right. In the photos, I could see little glimpses of me in her. After the photos were taken, we were given a memory box. They asked if we wanted Asya with us in the room where we would spend that night. We said yes. They explained they would take her after I was discharged. It was so quiet in our room that night. I cried myself to sleep.

I was discharged the next day, still weak. I had not eaten much in two days and those ice chips they gave me while in labor were no source of energy. Steve collected my things while I sat in a wheelchair that morning preparing to leave. He pushed me in the wheelchair outside the hospital doors where I sat while he went to get the car. Although the moment between me waiting for him and him returning with the car was brief, it was awful. I sat alone in that wheelchair with empty arms. Empty. Just before he pulled up to the curb where I was waiting, I happened to glance to my right and saw a new mommy with her arms full, holding her newborn all bundled up in a blanket. I turned away as the tears started flowing, again. I was heartbroken.

We spent the next several days at my folks' home. On the evening of the first day there, I mustered up the energy to get in the shower. I thought feeling refreshed physically might help me mentally. But not even a minute after the water hit my body, my milk started to come in. I could not believe it! My body was producing nourishment for the daughter who would never receive it. It was incredibly painful physically because I did not have a baby to nurse and it was painful emotionally because I did not have a baby to nurse. It was a fresh and tangible reminder of our devastating loss. The next day, I contacted my doctor and she told me to wear a bandage or bandeau to restrict the flow until the process ran its course. I felt like a truckload of salt had just been dumped on my wound.

Although that experience left me depleted and discouraged, I could not let go of my desire to be a mom. I started to rebuild my faith, meditating on God's promises. As soon as I received the green light later that year, we decided to use some of the eggs that had been retrieved during my fertility treatment months earlier but had not been implanted. Weeks after that second IVF procedure, I had an appointment with my doctor to determine whether I was pregnant. Steve met me at the doctor's office. Sadly, we learned I had a chemical pregnancy. My hormones were elevated, but there was no embryo. I was crushed, to say the least. Rather than have a dilation and curettage (D&C), a procedure to remove tissue from the uterus lining after a miscarriage or abortion, I decided to let the miscarriage occur naturally. I left that teary appointment incredibly disappointed. Steve had to go back to work. As a temporary distraction from the emotional pain at that moment, I decided to go shopping. I went to one of my favorite clothing stores in the outdoor shopping center next to the doctor's office and bought a white winter coat. After that purchase, I drove home feeling numb.

Within the hour, I started to miscarry. I cannot begin to put into words how intense the pain was. I mean, I could barely breathe! I sat on the landing of our staircase panting, and then slowly crawled up the stairs to our bedroom using the banister to help me pull myself forward. Once I got to the top of the steps, I rushed to the bathroom. I lay on the cold floor holding my abdomen then crawled to my bed and then dashed to the commode when the bleeding began in earnest. This went on for what felt like an eternity. When the miscarriage process was over, I just wanted to sleep. I lay on our bed in a fetal position, in silence, with the blinds closed. I needed stillness. I was completely drained physically and emotionally.

***

In the fall, my fertility specialist recommended I consider acupuncture. He explained that acupuncture has many benefits, including helping to reduce stress and improve circulation to the reproductive organs. Continuing to believe God can do anything and that I was meant to be a mommy, I was willing to try it. I found one of the city's leading integrative medical centers with a physician-led medical acupuncturist practice. The physicians and healthcare practitioners work with patients for a variety of ailments. I saw a wonderful OB-GYN who had studied alternative medicine and was practicing acupuncture there. Most of her patients were women suffering from infertility. I had acupuncture treatments for many months, and they were amazingly relaxing. I always left those appointments deeply rested, replenished, and in a good mental space. It was as though someone had dusted away some of the negative thoughts that had accumulated in my thought-life that week as I continued to push through my journey to motherhood. I felt like I was on the road to becoming fertile.

Just then a woman who had been subject to bleeding for twelve years came up behind him and touched the edge of his cloak.

She said to herself, "If I only touch his cloak, I will be healed."

Jesus turned and saw her. "Take heart, daughter," he said, "your faith has healed you." And the woman was healed at that moment.

— MATTHEW 9:20-22

CHAPTER FIVE

Course Correction

YEAR FOUR

Months went by and out of nowhere . . . well, I take that back, God helped me to recall the name of a reproductive endocrinology and infertility (REI) specialist a friend had told me about years earlier. Somehow, I learned about a seminar the specialist was giving on acupuncture and laparoscopy procedures. I decided to attend and introduced myself after his presentation. I briefly explained our fertility woes, and he invited me to schedule an appointment. He also asked me to have my medical records sent to his office as soon as possible. I scheduled the appointment and Steve and I met with him. He said that after reviewing all of my medical records (I was extremely impressed that he had reviewed my records before our first appointment!), he did not see where endometriosis had been ruled out as a cause of my infertility. I had heard of endometriosis, but it never occurred to me to consider it as the culprit for my infertility or to even discuss the condition with my doctors. Sadly, none of the specialists I had seen those last few years mentioned this condition as something we should explore.

Up until this point, my diagnosis had been along the lines of "unexplained infertility." I chalked it up to my age. By this time, I was knocking on the door of the big 4-0. After discussing endometriosis and treatment options, Steve and I prayed about it and decided I would undergo laparoscopic excision surgery. The surgery revealed I had stage III endometriosis, which included the presence of a benign cyst. My surgery was in September. One month later I turned forty. I thought about my age at the time and had a sobering moment. I realized that I was eighteen years old when my mom was forty. Yet, here I was forty years old and still not a mom. That was a tough reality, but I could not allow that to render me hopeless. I still desired to become a mom and held onto my faith.

Now faith is confidence in what we hope for and assurance about what we do not see.

— HEBREWS 11:1

CHAPTER SIX

The Going Just Got Tougher

YEAR FIVE

In January of that next year, I discovered a love for spinning. Albeit that hard bicycle seat took some getting used to, I started incorporating it into my exercise regime. I also began fertility yoga classes offered at my REI's office. Fertility yoga is designed to help women nurture, support, and strengthen their reproductive systems so that they can conceive a child. It can help increase blood flow to reproductive organs. And equally important for me, it helped lower my stress level, something many women are consumed by when they have been on this journey for a while. My stress level was at a 10, and I realized that it was critical for me to do whatever it took to boost my mental well-being. I continued to take my prescription prenatal vitamins. I even added an Omega-3 supplement to my routine. Although I had not been pregnant in over a year, I wanted to keep my now forty-year-old body healthy for my future baby. I also faithfully tracked my menstrual cycle. So when I realized I was a few days late a little over a month into the new year, I called my REI doctor's office immediately to schedule an appointment. *Could I be pregnant?* I wondered. I wanted a definitive answer. No over-the-counter pregnancy test would suffice. I wanted a blood test. A day after the test, I got the call from the nurse. She told me I was pregnant. It was hard to believe, but I became pregnant naturally for the first time ever! We were on cloud nine, although, admittedly, I was scared too. We thanked God. Motherhood was my destiny and so I refused to drown in our heartbreak and disappointments. We had still been praying that the Lord would bless us with a child from my womb.

My REI doctor saw me a few days later and then a few weeks later. Having been weeks into my pregnancy by this next appointment, he told me I would see a little light flashing on the monitor—our baby's heartbeat. It is hard to express how excited I was to see that little light! I think I was still shocked that I was actually pregnant.

Before I left, I made another appointment to see my REI doctor in a few weeks. Because his office was across the street from my job, I had planned most of my appointments during lunch. Since Steve had not been able to accompany me on those appointments up until that point, I scheduled my next appointment for Saturday. My husband was going to preach the message at church that Saturday morning, so I made the appointment very early that day.

We arrived at my REI doctor's office, and I changed into the gown before my doctor came in the exam room. He began the ultrasound. Just a few seconds later, he pushed his chair back from the exam table. I could see his eyes were starting to look watery. Then he simply said, "I'm sorry."

We lost our baby! I was about ten weeks pregnant. Although I was still in my first trimester, we had already begun to love our baby. As soon as my pregnancy was confirmed, it was like a switch automatically triggered in my heart. I was instantly in love with my baby, the baby whose heartbeat was evidenced only by a light. We were crushed. I do not remember what we said to each other as we drove home. Steve put on his suit and left for church. I, on the other hand, could not pull myself together to get dressed to go.

I was confused. I mean, I understood what my doctor told

me, but I did not understand why it was happening. Why had we suffered this loss? Only two couples and another friend knew we were pregnant. They had been praying for us and encouraging us throughout our road to parenthood, starting when we began fertility treatments, the loss of our first daughter, and our journey following that loss. I called my friend Karen, the wife of one of those couples. She had rushed to our house the day we found out that we loss Asya. Once, again, she rushed over to be there in a time of need. She attends the same church and was about to leave when she received my call. She sat with me while I talked and cried. At one point while she was consoling me, I checked the time and popped off the couch and realized I had to go to church. I would not let Steve be there alone after receiving such devastating news. He was hurting too. I threw on a dress as fast as I could, and we raced out the door.

When we arrived at church, my husband was on the pulpit at the front of the church, on his knees, pouring out his heart in a very emotional prayer. I remember that he was literally crying out to God, saying that God knew he was burdened, sad, and did not want to be there. Then he concluded by saying he would serve God nonetheless! No one knew from where this anguish and pain was coming except the two couples and our friend who we had shared our loss earlier that morning. Through my own tears, I saw the husband of one of the couples a few pews in front of me crying. At that point, I wasn't sure if my husband was going to be able to preach after his prayer. But God used him. In fact, one of my friend's mother—neither of which knew about our loss—told my friend that she needed to get the DVD of his sermon because, in her opinion, it was one of the best messages he had ever preached. I had always respected my husband's faith and spiritual maturity, but that experience took my respect, love, and honor for him to a completely different level.

A few days after our loss, we saw my doctor and decided to have a D&C. The thought of waiting for the miscarriage to happen naturally was scary because I remembered how painful my miscarriage was years earlier. I also opted for the D&C because I wanted my doctor to examine some of my baby's tissue, which would be removed for genetic testing. I wanted to know if there was something wrong that could explain the miscarriage. There was. The procedure revealed that there was a chromosomal problem. We were saddened by the news, yet acknowledged that God knew what was best.

I was still very disappointed and emotionally drained.

Months passed and I wondered when it would happen for me. And in October, my birthday month, I received the best gift ever—I was pregnant! For the second time, conception occurred with no medical assistance. We had not stopped praying and asking God to answer our prayers for a child. We had been claiming His promises and strengthening our faith. We shared our good news with a few friends who had continued supporting us in prayer. We also told immediate family. We were planning to tell the extended family in a few days during the annual Thanksgiving celebration at my folks'. This is my dad's favorite holiday, which means my siblings and their families all gather for four to five days of holiday festivities. At the time, my grandmother was eighty-six years old and lived in a nearby senior retirement home. Because her birthday was November 22nd, which falls on Thanksgiving Day some years, we always celebrated her birthday on Thanksgiving. Steve and I were excited to have another reason to celebrate with our family. But days before Thanksgiving, we lost the pregnancy. I was emotionally battered by this time. Hopes dashed, dreams unfulfilled. I just could not understand why this happened again. I mean, my husband and I were married, he had been a faithful servant of God since he was eighteen. We were not perfect, but we were His children. I could not understand why we were still on this journey of disappointment. I called my dad to tell him the news the day before Thanksgiving. I told him I did not want to come for the holiday, but that I would. When we got to my family's house, I did not want to talk about our loss. I was frustrated, mad, and disheartened. There was nothing anyone could say that would make me feel better.

Still committed to exhausting every feasible option we could, in December, we saw my REI doctor to discuss whether I should undergo a myomectomy to have my uterine fibroids removed. We knew I had fibroids, but the location of the ones my doctor could see and feel were not in my uterine cavity (submucous) and did not appear to decrease my fertility. We prayed about it. We knew recovery from a myomectomy would be four to six weeks. But we wanted to know in our hearts that we did everything we could. I was meant to be a mother and would not let Satan persuade me to doubt that fact. I was still standing on God's promises and meditating on His Word daily.

When you are fighting a battle, you must arm yourself with the sword of life—God's Word. Cited from the New International Version (NIV) of the Holy Bible, the following are some of the Bible verses I held onto in my heart and mind during my fertility battle:

I prayed for this child, and the Lord has granted me what I asked of him.
— 1 SAMUEL 1:27

Children are a heritage from the Lord, offspring a reward from him.
— PSALM 127:3

Your wife will be like a fruitful vine within your house; your children will be like olive shoots around your table.
— PSALM 128: 3

This is the confidence we have in approaching God: that if we ask anything according to his will, he hears us.

And if we know that he hear us— whatever we ask—we know that we have what we asked of him.
— 1 JOHN 5:14-15

Let us hold unswervingly to the hope we profess, for he who promised is faithful.
— HEBREWS 10:23

Just then a woman who had been subject to bleeding for twelve years came up behind him and touched the edge of his cloak.
She said to herself, "If I only touch his cloak, I will be healed."

Jesus turned and saw her. "Take heart, daughter," he said, "your faith has healed you." And the woman was healed at that moment.
— MATTHEW 9:20-22

For the Spirit God gave us does not make us timid, but gives us power, love, and self-discipline.

— 2 TIMOTHY 1:7

Dear friend, I pray that you may enjoy good health and that all may go well with you, even as your soul is getting along well.

— 3 JOHN 2

He will love you and bless you and increase your numbers. He will bless the fruit of your womb, and the crops of your land—your grain, new wine and olive oil—the calves of your herds and the lambs of your flocks in the land he swore to your ancestors to give you.

— DEUTERONOMY 7:13

These Bible verses were like life preservers that helped me stay afloat, that kept me above water and not drowning in the sea of stress and hopelessness of infertility. There is power in His Word. I am a witness!

We decided I would have the procedure and scheduled it for December 27th, right after Christmas, but before the new year when I would face a new deductible on my high-deductible health plan. Yes, I had to think about insurance and money while fighting for my fertility, in faith!

CHAPTER SEVEN

Not Giving Up

YEAR SIX

A s the new year began, I was healing from my myomectomy and eager to get the green light to start trying to conceive. We tried for several months and nothing happened. Because I conceived twice without any fertility medications or procedures, my anxiousness to become a mother was in overdrive. But each month I menstruated, I had to face the brutal reality that I was not pregnant. Yet, through my feelings of disappointment, tears, heartache, and frustration, I would not accept that I was not going to become pregnant. It was hard. But I had to make a concerted effort to not allow myself to be consumed by a tornado of pessimism when I thought about how heartbreaking our fertility journey had been up to that point. I would remind myself that I still had an opportunity because I was still menstruating. While that metaphoric Bong I heard years ago had reached its peak, I decided I would continue to claim God's promises and inundate my heart and mind with the Bible verses I mentioned.

You have to make a deliberate decision to have faith. I distinctly recall sitting in our car in a friend's driveway as we were about to get out and have lunch at her house. I wish I could remember the date. But that afternoon, I remember telling my husband that I had to make a decision—I had to decide that I was going to believe or not believe that God would answer my prayer. I could not waiver in my belief. I could regard our previous losses, the negative reports from my two D&C procedures, and the fact that I was now forty-one (approaching forty-two in a few short months) as legitimate and logical reasons for feeling hopeless about my getting pregnant and giving birth. I could believe that it was simply just too difficult for the Creator of everything to create life in me, one of His creations. He told the woman who was subject to bleeding for twelve years that "your faith has healed you" (Matthew 9:22, NIV). That meant it was not about my husband's faith, my pastor's faith, or the faith of our friends and family. It was about *my* faith: "Now faith is confidence in what we hope for and assurance about what we do not see" (Hebrews 11:1, NIV). Either I would believe it regardless of how things looked or I would not. I remembered Hebrews 11:1 and chose to believe!

Let's be honest, having faith while in the midst of a difficult situation is not easy. However, it is a choice to believe God and His power to do anything or to not believe. Either way, you believe something. A few years earlier, we sold our home and temporarily moved into an apartment. One day while packing for the move, I saw my box of maternity clothes. I also saw the baby swing we received as a gift during our first pregnancy, through IVF, just a year earlier. I felt sick to my stomach seeing these things because I was reminded afresh of our stillborn daughter. I contemplated whether we should keep the swing. But Steve said we would, and he put it in our storage area. Now I know he kept it in faith. A year later, we purchased another house and I saw the swing and maternity clothes. My husband loaded the items on the moving truck, once again, and we stored them in our new home.

Then I remembered the vision my sweet friend Candace said God had given her, which she shared with us about two years after our stillbirth. In the vision, we had given birth to a baby girl and we were at church at our daughter's baby blessing. She and her husband had traveled to town to join us at the blessing because, by that time, they had relocated to another state. Now, at the time Candace shared this with us, we all lived in the same city and she had no plans to move. She reminded us of her vision even a year after she first told us. On more than one occasion, I would recall her vision in a moment of discouragement, in a moment when I could barely hang on to God's promises, when I could feel my faith under attack by Satan's persistent reminder of all we had loss and the very real fact that I was, undeniably, years into the advance maternal age category. I believe God was speaking through her, telling me to not give up, that the effectual and fervent prayer avails much, that He could do anything, including creating and sustaining life in my womb. We also had people praying for us all over the country, literally. I remember one evening Steve had his phone on speaker while requesting prayer on his weekly prayer line. I was moved to tears hearing one of the men of God pray for us. It gave me strength. There really is power in prayer!

We continued to pray and started trying to conceive as soon as I completely healed from my myomectomy.

But nothing happened. Month after month, my period arrived right on time. I was so disappointed. Sometimes I would have a crying session, often while reading God's promises. Tears would roll down my cheeks. Sometimes I could barely see what I was reading because my vision would be blurred from my tears. I had moments when I was just mad that I was going through this. Why me, why us? I would ask God what was wrong with me. But after those sessions, I would pull myself together. I would speak life because I could not accept that I would not have a child. I determined in my heart to believe God even when I did not feel like believing God.

CHAPTER EIGHT

The Best Christmas Gift Ever!

YEAR SEVEN

nother year came and went and we still did not have our bundle of joy. By now, I was forty-two. Yes, I said forty-two! I would be less than honest if I did not admit that number seemed daunting when I thought about the fact that I was still on this long, frustrating, and heartbreaking journey. I was well past the advanced maternal age of thirty-five where the statistics on having a healthy baby are simply not favorable and, truly scary. But I refused to let Satan have the last word.

I continued taking my prescription prenatal vitamins. By this point, I often felt silly and embarrassed when I would pick up the prescription because I always had to verify my date of birth. I just knew that pharmacist had quickly calculated how old I was and was thinking, *What is she thinking?! Doesn't she know she is forty-two? Hello!* But I faithfully got that prescription filled years before I became pregnant with Symone. I told myself that I had to do everything I could to make sure my body was healthy to carry a healthy baby regardless of what those stats indicated. I continued taking my DHA Omega-3 prenatal supplement, which supports brain development. The brand I used was not sold in stores, but by independent business owners. One of my coworkers was an owner, and I bought them from her. For months, I would place my order, yet my belly was not growing. I remember thinking many times that she had to be wondering why I was taking the supplement. But the Bible tells us, "Now faith is confidence in what we hope for and assurance about what we do not see" (Hebrews 11:1, NIV). So, I continued to prepare my body for the baby I was praying for.

Satan is a liar. I knew I was meant to be a mother and refused to question that truth even when things were not going as planned. Yes, I got bold because I was inundating my mind and heart with the Word. I had to believe that God would answer my prayer and not just that He *could* answer my prayer. Again, He said, "your faith has healed you," which meant it was according to my faith (Matthew 9:22, NIV).

While still praying, Steve and I began discussing adoption

that February. I was ready to begin the role of mommy. He started researching adoption agencies, and we narrowed our choice to a local, private agency. We completed the necessary paperwork and made a nominal payment toward the services we would receive during the adoption process. But unlike what some people say to prospective adoptive parents, I did not relax thinking, finally, I will be a mom soon. No! I became even more intense and bold in my prayers.

Adoption is a wonderful opportunity and a blessing to parents and children alike. But I wanted to be pregnant again. I wanted my husband to see my belly growing, I wanted him to rub my belly in that affectionate and loving way he did when I was pregnant with Asya, I wanted to wear my maternity clothes, and I was willing to fight through my morning sickness, again, if it meant the blessing of feeling a little life moving in my womb. So while we were reading the book about adoption assigned in the class, I was still reading and meditating and claiming, in faith, His promises about children. I was praying and asking the Lord to please answer my prayers.

After completing our classes, we scheduled our first home study two months later, that April. We met with the social worker from the adoption agency at our kitchen table. I do not remember her name, but I do recall she had a kind spirit. She reviewed the process with us and talked about the packet of documents we needed to complete. We also started to discuss some of our assigned reading. The meeting lasted about an hour. We ended by discussing next steps and said we would see her at our next scheduled meeting as we walked her to the door. Steve had already started making his way upstairs as I closed our front door. Before he reached the top of that last step, I exclaimed, "I think I'm pregnant!"

He quickly stopped, turned around with a surprised look on his face, and excitedly asked, "What?!"

I said again, "I think I'm pregnant!" I told him that my period was a few days late. I was very regular during that period of time (no pun intended!) so I knew I was late. I had not mentioned to him the first day that I was late because I wanted to protect his emotions, and I wanted one or two more days to pass before confirming. I do not remember how many days I was late, but I remember I could not hold it in anymore . . . I had to tell him. I also told him I would call my REI doctor the next day to try to get an appointment for a blood test. There was no way I was going to rely on an over-the-counter pregnancy test. I needed to know, for certain, if I was pregnant. He agreed.

I was able to get an appointment the next day, which was April 27th. Due to the time of my appointment, I was told my results would not be available until the following day. That was the longest twenty-four hours. But, on April 28th, the nurse called me from my REI's office. When I answered, she asked, "Is this Kim Garner?"

"Yes!" I replied eagerly and with anticipation.

And then she said those four beautiful words, "You are very pregnant!" I could not believe it! I was elated! She congratulated me and told me to come for an appointment the next day. I hung up the phone and called Steve as quickly as I could with the good news. We received confirmation of my pregnancy on April 28th, which was exactly one day before our tenth wedding anniversary! We were planning to leave for vacation in a few days to celebrate this milestone. Now we had even more to celebrate!

That evening, and the days following, Satan started to do his thing. My miscarriages and previous D&C outcomes began to flood my mind. My joy started to be tainted with fear. Immediately, I began to attack those negative thoughts like my life depended on it. Daily, sometimes multiple times during the day, I would remind myself of His promises. Two of my favorite Bible verses are in the Book of John:

This is the confidence we have in approaching God: that if we ask anything according to his will, he hears us.

And if we know that he hears us— whatever we ask—we know that we have what we asked of him.

— 1 JOHN 5:14-15

I also held close to my heart these Bible verses:

Forget the former things; do not dwell on the past.

See I am doing a new thing! Now it springs up; do you not perceive it? I am making a way in the wilderness and streams in the wasteland.

— ISAIAH 43:18-19

Yes, I thought, *God will do a new thing!* I told myself that my previous losses were not the end of our story. I started to really acknowledge that Satan is a loser, and he knows it. This is why we must trust God. His Word is a shelter and comfort. His Word is power. And I am not saying this because it sounds good. I am saying it because I know it to be true. I lived it. It is my testimony! And trusting requires that you remain aware of your thought-life. "...Whatever is pure, whatever is lovely, whatever is admirable . . . think about such things" (Philippians 4:8, NIV). To me, that meant I had to make a deliberate and intentional effort to not stay in the valley of hopelessness, regardless of past disappointments. I had to look forward. I had to control my thoughts and not allow them to control me.

Once we soaked in the excitement of our pregnancy, we shared our news with our family and a small circle of friends who had supported us throughout our journey to become parents. Next, we started discussing what we should tell the adoption agency. We needed to think about whether to discontinue the process. I must admit, I was nervous. I thought, *What if I lose this pregnancy too?!* I was disappointed in myself that I had that thought, yet I did. But then I made a conscious, deliberate decision to not live in fear. I made a conscious, deliberate decision to claim His promises, in faith. And so we shared our news with the owner of the adoption agency. She was happy for us. She understood what this meant because not only did she own the agency, but she was also an adoptive mother of two little girls. She understood the deep pain of infertility firsthand, which was one of the reasons we were persuaded to work with her agency. We told her we were putting our adoption plans on hold. Although we had our first home study in the adoption process, we had not been matched with a birthmother at this point.

Let me just say that the battle was real! Satan launched a Herculean effort to paralyze me into a hopeless state of fear. He tried to persuade me that I was too old to carry and deliver a healthy baby—by this time I was forty-two years old. He reminded me that I never carried a child full-term. He reminded me of Asya. He reminded me that I lost the pregnancies that occurred without fertility treatment because of chromosomal problems. Simply put, he tried to discourage me like none other. It is in times like that it is a blessing to know God's promises. I did my best to counter every negative thought with God's Word. That was the only way I could make it!

Before I began having monthly appointments with my OB, I saw my REI doctor several times. Often, I would read or recite some encouraging Bible verses before my appointment to quell my nervousness. I was in such a battle, fighting for my baby. I did the same thing with each prenatal visit with my OB. At my first appointment this time around, she sensed my anxiety. Before I left her office that day, I will never forget how she gently put her hands on my shoulders, looked me in my eyes, and said, in a reassuring way, "Everything will be OK." She said she became a doctor for moments like this and then hugged me. God used her for me that day. He knows when the comfort of another is what you need at the very moment you need it.

As my pregnancy progressed, we were faced with the decision whether or not to have an amniocentesis procedure as with our precious Asya. At my core, I wanted the procedure because I wanted to hear the doctor say everything was okay. But Steve asked what we would do with the test results whether they were positive or negative. What if we received inaccurate information? Or what if we were correctly told that the results indicated there was a health issue with our baby? Abortion was not an option for us, so having the information would only serve to cause anxiety during the pregnancy. I prayed and asked God to please direct us in this decision. With the risks involved with an amniocentesis, I felt God encouraging me to not have the procedure. And so I declined.

Because an amniocentesis is generally done between weeks 15 and 20 of a pregnancy, there was no changing my mind after the window closed for the procedure. It was one of the hardest decisions I have ever made even though I felt impressed to make the decision. I cried a little. I wanted the doctor to tell me my baby was perfect, in superb health based on the test results. However, God reminded me about Hebrews 11:1, "Now faith is confidence in what we hope for and assurance about what we do not see." And then Mark 5:34, "He said to her, 'Daughter, your faith has healed you. Go in peace and be freed from your suffering.'" I had to trust God to tell me that everything would be okay. Those months were a faith walk unlike any I had ever experienced. Each day I asked the Lord to give me strength, to not allow negative thoughts to consume me. I had to renew my faith daily. It was tough!

I was extremely in tune with my body. I would make a mental note about when I felt our baby move. I would ask God to please protect our baby and began to pray specific prayers over our baby. First, I prayed for a daughter. The Lord says to be specific and so I was specific. Next, throughout my pregnancy,

I prayed over our baby's development: brain cells, heart, lungs, fingers, toes, sight, hearing, smell, taste, amygdala, circulatory system, reproductive system, nervous system, thyroid, small and large intestines, kidneys, shoulder blades, knees, thighs, shins, calves, hamstring muscles, buttocks, back—I called out every part of the body I could think of during those prayer sessions.

Besides the morning sickness that dogged me every day, all day, my pregnancy progressed well. As the date for my twenty-week appointment got closer, I was excited to find out the gender. I was also a little tense because the last time I saw my OB while twenty weeks pregnant I was heartbroken. I started to feel that heartbreak anew. Yet, again, I looked to His promises to keep me.

The night before the twenty-week prenatal appointment, I remember peeping into the room we selected for the baby's nursery. I almost started to cry because Steve was setting up the baby swing—the swing we received as a gift four years earlier from the registry we created when I was pregnant with Asya, the swing that we had loaded and unloaded during our last two moves. The swing was unmistakably a baby girl's swing—pink and white. I remember talking to God that night in prayer and reiterating that He please, please let us have a baby girl. It sounds silly now, but in that prayer, I shared with God that He had to give us a baby girl because we had the girl swing and I just could not put a baby boy in it!

Finally, the big day arrived—ultrasound day. As Steve and I walked into the ultrasound room, my heart was pounding. I started feeling uneasy so I reminded myself that God created this life and began silently reciting some of His promises I had been meditating on. The technician began the exam by squeezing the ultrasound gel on my belly. I was pleasantly surprised at how warm the gel was. Next, she slowly rolled the transducer across my uterus. Within seconds, I nearly jumped off the table when I veered to the right and saw my baby moving on the monitor! The last time I looked at a monitor like that was four years earlier, and my baby girl was lifeless, seemingly suspended in my amniotic fluid. This time I could see my busy little bee squirming around. All I could think in that moment was God is good!

The technician continued gliding the transducer across my uterus, and I could hear a clicking sound. I asked what that was and she said she was measuring the baby's body and organs. While she was measuring, I was nearly bursting at the seams because I wanted to know what we were having, a boy or a girl. I was on the table for what felt like hours and still didn't know the gender of my baby. Up to this point during the exam, the technician used the definitive article "the" each time she referred to the baby. Politely, yet anxiously, I asked, "Can you tell the sex of the baby?"

She casually replied, "I think so." That was it. She did not elaborate at all. Now, I was thinking, *What do you mean you think so?! Are you going to tell me?!*

I ask, as calmly as I could, "What do you think?"

"I think you are having a girl," she said.

I asked her if she was sure, and she said she was fairly certain. I could barely contain my excitement. She continued the exam while I screamed inside, overjoyed and thanking God. She said our daughter looked healthy. However, because she was squirming so much, the technician told me I needed to come back in about a week for her to take another measurement of the heart chamber because she wanted to make sure she got it right. Fear gripped me momentarily, *Oh no! Is there something wrong with her heart?* But then I decided I wouldn't read more into it and trust God.

While waiting for my next appointment that same afternoon,

this time with my OB, I called my dad but could not reach him. Next, I called my stepmother. I told her she was going to have a granddaughter. There was a brief pause on the phone. I don't remember what she said verbatim, but I remember she was crying while talking. I got off the phone when the nurse called me back to the exam room. It was a wonderful appointment. I listened to my daughter's heartbeat. It was absolutely the best sound ever! I was simply overwhelmed with joy. I was having a daughter! My OB was very excited about our news.

I continued to see my OB monthly. Once I reached the third trimester, my prenatal visits became more frequent and much longer. I essentially had three appointments in one. First, I had an ultrasound. Next, I was hooked up to a machine that graphed my daughter's heartbeat for about 20 minutes. Finally, I saw my OB. I didn't mind the nearly hour-long appointments. I was willing to do whatever it took to get through the pregnancy and deliver a healthy baby.

Shortly after we found out we were having a baby girl, Steve and I started discussing names. For the rest of my pregnancy, we wanted to call her name specifically when we prayed over her while in my womb. I always had an affinity for French culture and thought I would check out some names on a

French baby name website. The name Simone caught my eye. I thought it was perfect because I wanted our daughter's name to begin with an "S" like my husband's name. That evening I shared the name with Steve. He said he liked it, but said we first needed to find out the meaning. And he was right. We learned that in Hebrew Simone means "she who hears, God has heard." That sealed the deal. But I decided I didn't want to spell it "Simone" with an "i." I thought if anyone inadvertently left the "e" off the end, her name would read as "Simon." For some reason, that bothered me. When I saw the name spelled as "Symone," I asked my husband what he thought. He liked it. We decided that "Symone" was perfect. We made a promise to each other to explain to our daughter the meaning of her name. We want her to know that like many women in the Bible (e.g., Sarah and Elizabeth), God heard our prayers for her life. And we pray that her name will forever remind her that God honors faith and answers prayers. We want her to know that nothing is too hard for God. Her very life is a testimony and witness to that truth.

As my pregnancy progressed, my dear friend Karen got a group of my friends together to plan the best baby shower a mom-to-be could dream of. The morning of the celebration, the baby shower planning crew descended upon our house with an assortment of boxes and bags overflowing with stuff. Before I could find out what I needed to do, Joan and Kawanna, two close friends who had flown into town for the weekend, scooted me upstairs to root through my closet to find a cute outfit. I could not figure out what to wear and had thrown on some jeans and a random top. Clearly, it looked like I had been struggling because they kindly suggested I change. Once they coordinated my outfit and I was fully dressed and prepped, I did a quick hair check and dashed back downstairs to ask what I could do.

Karen flatly rejected my invitation to help. Instead, my two "stylists" kicked me out of my house and took me to breakfast. I enjoyed catching up with my girls because I had not seen them in a while. I also tried to leverage that time by peppering them with questions about the shower. I wanted details about who was coming, the decorations, the menu . . . everything. They would not budge. The more I pressed, the bigger they grinned. I was forced to wait and just enjoy the girlfriend time and my scrumptious French toast and eggs on my plate.

We chatted for awhile after we finished our food until they received the call that we could head back to my house.

Unsure about what surprises awaited, I gingerly opened my front door. My friends were eager to capture my reaction and hurried me inside. The aroma of homemade quiche and buttery yeast rolls made from scratch greeted us at the door. Although I had eaten less than an hour ago, my taste buds were at full attention. Before I could close the door, I was enveloped by the melodies of French classical music playing throughout the house. I imagined I was strolling into a quaint French café tucked away on a Parisian cobblestone street. I continued walking through my foyer and spotted hot pink glittered letters that spelled Symone. Yes, I was tickled pink by this time!

All the baby shower decorations were simply delightful. Perched on the mantel of our fireplace was a huge poster of the Eiffel tower. Baby onesies dangled from classic wooden clothespins on a wire that was strung across our family room windows. Symone's name was on a white, two-tiered cake garnished with edible pearls my close friend had baked. I was impressed—I had no idea my Ana had such baking skills.

As if it wasn't enough that Karen spearheaded the planning and execution of the shower, she sewed French-inspired aprons for all of my friends who assisted in the planning.

They were super cute! But her creativity and vision didn't end there. She designed the chair I sat on while opening my gifts, which she had found at a second-hand store and spiced up. She purchased some pink and white gingham material to sew a cushion cover for the chair and painted the chair's wooden frame white, incorporating a pop of pink and chartreuse on the chair legs. She adorned the top of the seat back with a wooden piece in the shape of the fleur-de-lis, a stylized version of an iris, which is France's national flower. Karen also had a little riser constructed by another friend's husband. My custom-designed chair was center stage on the riser, which is where I sat when it was time for me to open each adorable baby gift.

My French-themed baby shower was magnifique! I cannot put into words how much love was put into planning this special occasion for me and Steve. Our house was overflowing with friends from near and far. Not everyone knew all the details of our fertility journey, but they knew we lost our stillborn daughter and supported us emotionally and through prayer. When you are fighting for your fertility, or any long, difficult trial, you need people on your team who will pray for you. We were beyond blessed to have some prayer warriors on our team.

After my baby shower, I had to continue to remind myself of God's promises. I had moments where I thought how horrible it would be to have had such a lovely baby shower and to then lose the pregnancy. Yes, Satan was relentless in his efforts to discourage me. I had to combat each thought of fear with scripture. Our fertility journey gave me a new understanding of that saying, "There is power in His Word." It is true! His promises will strengthen your faith. Without faith, I would not have tried to get pregnant after our stillbirth and subsequent multiple miscarriages. Remember Hebrews 11:1, "Now faith is confidence in what we hope for and assurance about what we do not see." That means you believe that God can answer your prayer even when it appears to be too difficult or impossible.

Faith requires trusting in God. When you decide to trust God, you do so based on principle, based on who He is. It is not a decision based on feelings. It is like being married. Sometimes you may not "feel" like doing something if, for example, your spouse hurt your feelings or did not do something you asked. However, you make a decision to do so based on principle and because you love your spouse. I decided in my heart that I would trust God, regardless of how I felt about my past disappointments and the physical, emotional, and financial costs of our fertility journey. I decided to focus on who He is: The Creator of all things with all power. I read about how He answered the prayers of others. I recollected how He had answered prayers in my own life.

I believe it takes courage to have faith because you are trusting no matter how it looks at the time. Having faith may mean that someone you care about won't believe your faith will allow your desire to come to fruition. But it is your faith, not theirs. Do not allow yourself to think that preparing for the worst will prepare you for the worst. I implore you to claim His promises and expect a blessing because of your faith in the One who can do all things. It may be easier to give up. Do not!

***

A few months after my baby shower, Symone's nursery was furnished, the walls painted, and all her tiny onesies, clothes, blankets, and bibs washed and organized in her drawers. We had all the baby gear, including a breast pump. The car seat was installed and my hospital bag was packed. Now, all we were waiting for was our daughter. I was scheduled for a cesarean on December 28th. I was a little nervous, but extremely excited to meet her.

My last prenatal appointment before the big day was Thursday December 22nd. Because my REI doctor explained when I got pregnant that I would need to have a C-section due to prior surgeries and fibroids, and my OB agreed, I never had a vaginal exam to check my cervix during any of my prenatal visits. Due to a miscommunication at this last appointment, the nurse told me to get undressed and gave me a gown to put on before my OB saw me. When she came in the room and realized the miscommunication, she told me she did not have to check my cervix, as it was optional since I was scheduled to have the C-section in six days. My friend who was with me at this appointment told me flat out to not do it. She is a mother of three and knew firsthand that the exam was uncomfortable. However, I decided to have the check; I figured it would be okay. Oh, how wrong I was! I almost fell off the exam table. I took super deep breaths and held on to the side of the exam table. When it was over, I had to take an extra moment to compose myself. I should have listened to my friend!

During the check, my OB said I was three centimeters dilated. She offered to perform the C-section the next day, Friday, December 23rd. But I was scheduled to have the procedure the next week on the 28th. I wanted to wait for a special reason: my birthday is October 28th. That meant my daughter and I would be born on the same day of a month, although in different months. Symone, however, had different plans.

In the wee hours of Christmas morning, I got up to use the bathroom. It felt like the hundredth time in the last twenty-four hours. While on the commode, I heard a pop. I quickly hopped up and looked into the toilet, thinking that it might be the sound of the cervical plug I had read about. I made a visual inspection—I was not about to start swishing my hand in the water. I did not see anything unusual so I groggily climbed back in bed. Steve said I moaned off and on for about an hour. Finally, he tapped me and said we should call the doctor. We did.

The doctor on call asked whether I had any bleeding or spotting. He also asked how often the contractions were coming. Up until that point, I honestly had not thought about the fact that I might be having contractions. It had not crossed my mind that I could actually go into labor before my scheduled C-section in three short days. I thought I was just having some discomfort. I certainly was not thinking I was about to have a baby on Christmas morning. Hence, I had not timed anything, which is what Steve reported to the doctor. We were told to call back if the pain continued or if I noticed any bleeding. By now, I was pooped and tried to go back to sleep. I was still complaining about being in pain so Steve insisted we go to the hospital. Because we were planning to spend Christmas at my folks' house, I asked him to grab the Christmas gifts for my family and for each other under the tree in case this was a false alarm. I thought we would head to their house after a quick trip to the hospital to confirm all was well. Well, we did not make it to my folks' that morning.

The instant we got on the highway, the pain ramped up significantly. I mean, those contractions were intense. I was holding on to the side of the car trying to stabilize myself so I would not move as much while we raced down the highway. As soon as we zipped into the parking lot, I suggested to my husband that he drop me off at the emergency entrance before parking. I did not know where to go and figured this was an emergency situation. I waddled through the automatic doors and one of the individuals behind a small window asked what was wrong. I calmly said, "I think I am in labor." Someone quickly grabbed a wheelchair. A few minutes later, Steve came rushing in and followed the person wheeling me to the elevator. We went straight to the maternity wing. They put us in a room, and we waited for the nurse to come examine me. She did and told me my water had broke and that I was four to five centimeters dilated.

What?! I thought. I could not believe we were actually about to have a baby, and she was going to be born on Christmas Day! It hadn't occurred to me that Symone would come before my planned C-section. Several friends teased me near the end of my pregnancy, predicting I was going to have our daughter on Christmas. I always laughed it off, explaining I was having a C-section on December 28th, that she and I would share the same date of the month of our birth. Clearly, I was wrong!

Eventually, I was moved into triage where I begged for an epidural. I have an extremely low tolerance for pain and those contractions were leaving me breathless. Seeing the distress on my face, my sweet nurse flung the curtain open and darted out of triage on a mission to find an anesthesiologist to give me some relief. Because I knew early in my pregnancy that I had to have a C-section, I only took a class about how to care for a newborn—swaddling, diaper changes, bathing, etc. I did not take a Lamaze childbirth class to learn techniques for coping with the pain during labor. So as I was sitting on the edge of that table in triage desperately waiting for an epidural, I started to recount the scenes from different T.V. shows and movies I had seen where moms-to-be in labor were focusing on their breathing.

The nurse had me hooked up to a monitor and told me when the next contraction was coming so I could prepare to sync my breathing. That was rough! But her strategy helped until the anesthesiologist arrived. As soon as he pulled back the curtains in triage, and I mean as soon as he did, I blurted out, "Please do not let me see the needle!" I can barely handle seeing the needle used to draw blood at my annual physicals and knew a small glimpse of that epidural needle might put me over the edge. He obliged me. He explained what I would feel and told me to not move. I took a deep breath and he went for it. *Ahhhh,* the relief was nearly instantaneous. Slowly, I began to relax and calm my nerves.

Finally, after seven years—after surgeries, miscarriages, our stillbirth—the time had come to meet Symone! I reflected, *Whoa! I am about to have a baby!* A few of the nurses gently rolled my hospital bed down the hall to the operating room. I started to feel nervous. I was also a little disappointed because my OB, the one who had delivered our first daughter and had taken excellent care of me during this pregnancy, was not on call on Christmas. She was scheduled to be in the hospital in three days, on Wednesday, December 28th, for my *scheduled* C-section. After all I had experienced with her, I was saddened that she was not going to deliver Symone. Instead, I was in the care of the on-call doctor whom I had never met. He was in the same practice as my OB, but I had no history with him.

There was a flurry of activity in that operating room. They shifted me from the hospital bed to the operating table, one of the nurses erected a small sheet to block my view of the lower half of my body, and the nurses and doctors conferred with one another. I soon diverted my attention to the incredible nauseous feeling that had suddenly overwhelmed me while lying on the operating table. I whispered to the nurse that I felt sick and needed to vomit. I thought she did not hear me because she did not respond with a sense of urgency by quickly attempting to sit me up and put a bag or something in front of my mouth. *Oh my goodness,* I thought, *I am going to choke on my vomit!* But seconds later, she came to my side and told me to turn my head to the left. I did and vomited into the little dish she had placed right under my chin. And just like that, I was back to normal, well, relatively speaking.

Before the doctor began the surgery, he told me I would feel some tugging, but no pain. Because I was so concerned about whether the epidural was still working, he began to "test" its effectiveness. He touched me slightly, and I exclaimed, "I feel that!"

He said, "Okay," and touched me again.

And, again, I quickly blurted, "I feel that!" This went on for about one minute.

Finally, he stated I would feel his touch, but I would not feel any pain. Clearly, I was thinking I should not feel anything. In hindsight, I am certain I was annoying. The next day, I told one of my friends about this exchange. She laughed and said the epidural was a pain reliever, but it was not meant to paralyze me so, of course, I should feel a touch. Who knew?!

After the doctor thoroughly explained that I would feel something, but not pain, I tried to focus and relax. The medical staff began to take their positions around the operating table. Steve was sitting next to me, close to my head, and the doctors and nurses were on the other side of the sheet. I was not prepared for how anxious I would be. Feeling the doctor methodically move my organs around as he made his way to my daughter was a weird and unnerving feeling. I heard a buzzing noise coming from the surgical tool he used to cut through the layers of my abdomen. I could even smell something burning and asked was that me! I could barely breathe and wanted the C-section to be over. I can be heard on the video my husband recorded on his cell phone saying, "Please hurry! Please hurry!"

Steve kept reassuring me that everything was going well. And I remember him telling me, "They are almost finished honey, they are almost finished!" It was hard to believe that I was living that very moment. I was about to have a baby after seven long years of trying to become a mommy. Suddenly, in the middle of all the pulling and tugging, I finally heard the sweetest, most amazing sound ever . . . my daughter crying! Symone was here! I became a mommy at 7:42 a. m. on Christmas morning! I remember kind of gasping and then tears streaming down my face the moment I heard her cry. I felt like I was having an out-of-body experience. *"We just had a baby!"* I screamed inside.

I can be heard on the video asking, "How does she look?! How does she look?!" I was not asking because I wanted to know who she looked like. I was asking because I had been fervently praying for a healthy baby—no Down syndrome or other health issues. As I shared earlier, I declined the amniocentesis even though I was forty-two when I got pregnant with Symone. I had contemplated having the procedure because I wanted my doctor to tell me that everything was fine. But we decided to trust God 100 percent and opted to not have the procedure. So when my husband who, by this time, had followed the nurses to the other side of the operating room where they were weighing and examining Symone, said she was perfect, that was all I needed to hear.

I honestly think the anxiety of the morning and my emotions about our entire fertility journey overcame me because, after hearing his assuring words, the next thing I saw was my dad holding his only granddaughter in my recovery room. I do not remember holding Symone immediately after she was born, I do not remember saying anything else to Steve, I do not even remember being wheeled out of the operating room to the recovery room. I was o-u-t o-f i-t!

God had answered the prayer that only He could answer. By the time I delivered our daughter, I was a forty-three-year-old woman who had suffered a stillbirth and multiple miscarriages. Yet, I decided to not let go of my faith in Him and to really believe He can do anything. I refused to allow Satan to keep me from my blessing. God brought life into my life when Symone was born. Although the statistics were not in my favor to get pregnant naturally and have a healthy baby, God said yes! After seven years, seven being the number of completion in the Bible, and on the day we celebrate Jesus' birth, God answered our prayers!

I prayed for this child, and the LORD has granted me what I asked of him.

— 1 SAMUEL 1:27

CHAPTER NINE

Blessed

Because Steve and I believe children are a gift from God, we knew we would have Symone blessed at church. We planned the baby blessing for May 12th. At that time, I did not realize that was Mother's Day weekend. But what a perfect date it was to celebrate what God had done, how He had answered my prayer to give birth to a healthy daughter. I also thought about the fact that I had not attended church on Mother's Day weekend since my mother had died ten years earlier. I attend church nearly every week because I enjoy worshipping and praising God and the fellowship of other believers. It is very rare for me to miss church. But I had not gone on Mother's Day weekend since I lost my beautiful mom because it was simply too painful to hear a message about mothers and motherhood without my mom in my life. And the stillbirth and miscarriages I had suffered made that day even more unbearable.

As we began planning for a luncheon at our house after the baby blessing, we started making our guest list. It was at that moment God reminded me about the vision my friend Candace had several years before of her returning from out of town to attend our baby girl's blessing. On the weekend of the blessing, she and her husband drove from Tennessee where they had relocated a year or so earlier to join us for the baby blessing. When we recounted the vision over that weekend, the vision that God undeniably gave her, we cried tears of joy because it was a powerful reminder that God is so faithful.

Jesus looked at them and said, "With man this is impossible, but with God all things are possible."

— MATTHEW 19:26

CHAPTER TEN

Nothing is Impossible with Him

Our energetic, funny, observant, intelligent, independent, songbird, Christmas-birthday girl is full of life. We enrolled her in kindergarten at a private Christian school when she was four and a half years old despite her pediatrician telling us she doubted Symone would be able to start that year because she would not be five by the end of September. We prayed about it and God said she was ready. Symone thrived in kindergarten. She was in a multi-grade class of kindergartners and first graders, and her teacher had her doing some first-grade level work. Please understand that I am sharing this as evidence that God can answer your prayer in a way that far exceeds your prayer request. Ephesians 3:20 says, "Now to him who is able to do immeasurably more than all we ask or imagine, according to his power that is at work within us." I prayed for a healthy baby girl. The stats were not in my favor because I was no spring chickadee. But not only did God bless our daughter with good health, He blessed her mind.

What is even more exciting is that Symone really enjoys church. She participates in service (e. g., she has prayed up front, given the welcome, etc.) and is involved in a Christian children's club designed to teach children about God, family, and community. She can recite many Bible verses and knows several Bible stories. And Symone is such a songbird, constantly singing her favorite Christian songs. Together we have a good time during our family worship at home every day. When reading the Bible or one of her Bible story books in the evening, one of us usually sits in the chair Karen designed for my baby shower; the chair is in Symone's room next to her bed. Or, if she wishes, my husband and I snuggle up with her in her bed while reading. We believe you must train up a child in the way they should go and, prayerfully, they will not depart from those ways when they become older (see Proverbs 22:6, NIV).

If you have doubts, if you are scared to believe God can bless you with the gift of a little life, that He can alter your infertility condition, that He can allow you to get pregnant and have a healthy, fearfully, and wonderfully made baby, then remember our journey. You must have faith regardless of how things look, how old you are, how many people around you are pregnant while you still are not, how many D&C's you have had, how many miscarriages you have suffered, how many stillborn babies you have delivered, how many years you have been trying to conceive, and what the statistics indicate. He told the woman with the bleeding condition, "your faith has healed you" (Matthew 9:22, NIV). As I shared previously, in Hebrew, our daughter's name means "she who hears, God has heard." In faith, we believed God would hear and answer our prayers. God can hear and answer your prayers. But you have to do more than just believe He *can*; you must believe that He *will*. Remember my testimony, remember Symone. "Now faith is confidence in what we hope for and assurance about what we do not see" (Hebrews 11:1, NIV). Have faith . . . do not lose hope!

Wherever you may be on your fertility journey, visit 7yearstosymone.com for inspiration and hope.

www.ingramcontent.com/pod-product-compliance
Lightning Source LLC
Chambersburg PA
CBHW060008050426
42448CB00028B/1952